Leader of the Pack

Lilly Golden

SCHOLASTIC INC.
New York Toronto London Auckland Sydney
Mexico City New Delhi Hong Kong Buenos Aires

Cover Photo
© Tim Davis/Corbis

Copyright © 2004 by Scholastic Inc.
All rights reserved. Published by Scholastic Inc.
Printed in the U.S.A.

ISBN 0-439-68391-2

SCHOLASTIC, READ 180, and associated logos and designs are trademarks and/or registered trademarks of Scholastic Inc.

LEXILE is a registered trademark of MetaMetrics, Inc.

3 4 5 6 7 8 9 10   23   12 11 10 09 08

Contents

Joe LeMonnier © Scholastic Inc.

Two men are hunting a wolf.
Is the wolf in danger?

Hunting for Wolves

A helicopter flew over a forest in Canada. Two men sat inside. They were looking down. One was flying the helicopter. The other was aiming a gun.

A black wolf pup ran out of the forest. The man with the gun leaned out of the helicopter. He took careful aim. Then he fired at the wolf.

Bam!

"Got him!" the man said.

The wolf lay on the ground. But he wasn't dead. The man with the gun was a **biologist**. And his gun didn't shoot a bullet. It shot a dart. The dart had a drug on it. The drug made the wolf go to sleep.

The helicopter landed. The men jumped out. The biologist put a tag on the wolf. It said "Wolf 2." The men put Wolf 2 in a cage. They loaded the cage into the helicopter. Then they took off.

What do you think the men are going to do with the wolf?

biologist a scientist who studies living things

Wolves once lived in the West.
Then the ranchers moved in.

2

Wanted: Wolves

The helicopter flew to Yellowstone National Park. That's a big park in the western part of the United States.

Hundreds of years ago, wolves lived in the area where Yellowstone is today. But then, in the 1800s, cattle **ranchers** moved to the area. They didn't want the wolves to kill their cattle. So they

ranchers people who raise cattle, sheep, or horses on large pieces of land

An adult wolf drags off the head of a deer it has just killed.

hunted the wolves.

Years later, that made a problem. By the 1990s, there were too many deer and elk eating all the grass in Yellowstone. Why? There were no wolves around to eat them!

People at the park had an idea. Bring wolves back to Yellowstone!

Wolf 2 arrives in Yellowstone.
Will he like his new home?

3

The Wolves Return

Fourteen wolves were brought to Yellowstone in 1995. Wolf 2 was one of them. At first, the wolves were kept in large cages. They had to get used to Yellowstone. Then they would be set free.

Wolves are great hunters. But they couldn't hunt when they were in cages. So workers fed them dead deer.

Once, a fox ran into a wolf cage. Bad move! The wolf ate it.

Finally, it was time to set the wolves free. But first, a radio collar was put on each wolf. The collars would keep track of where the wolves were.

A worker opened Wolf 2's cage. At first Wolf 2 didn't move. Then he took a step. He sniffed the air. Then he began to run. He ran slowly. Then he ran faster.

Wolf 2 was free!

Why were radio collars put on the wolves?

Wolf 2 and Wolf 7 start a new wolf pack. Will it survive?

4

Leaders of the Pack

Soon Wolf 2 started a new **pack** with a female wolf. She was called Wolf 7. She had also come from Canada. Their pack was the first pack in Yellowstone in more than 70 years!

The leader of a wolf pack is called the **alpha**. Most packs have an alpha male and an alpha female. Wolf 2 and Wolf 7

pack a group of wolves
alpha a leader of a wolf pack

Group Living
Wolves live in groups called packs.

Wolves live in packs. Each pack has 8 to 20 members. A pack has its own area, or **territory**. Like dogs, wolves mark their territory. They pee on it to show that it's theirs.

The pack leaders are the alpha male and female. In some packs, the female is in charge. In others, the male is. Alpha wolves choose where to live. They lead the hunt. Most of the time, only the alphas have pups. When alphas get old or hurt, younger wolves take over.

Here's an alpha female with her pups. Pups live in their parents' den for about two months.

territory an area of land
den the home of a wild animal

were the alphas in their pack.

Wolf 2 and Wolf 7 were a great team. They hunted together. If one got sick, the other brought food to the pack. One worker said, "Wolf 2 was a great hunter and a great **provider** for his pups."

In six years, Wolf 2 and Wolf 7 raised 39 pups! As the pups grew up, they learned how to hunt. Then they became adults. And they started their own packs.

How did Wolf 2 and Wolf 7 work together?

provider someone or something that brings things that are needed

Wolf Hunt!

Here's how wolves get their food.

The pack is hungry. It's time to hunt. The wolves get together. They howl to greet each other. They also howl to keep other wolves away.

Next, the wolves look for animals to hunt. They might hunt elk, deer, moose, buffalo, or rabbits. They try to find an animal that is old, sick, or hurt.

When the wolves find an animal, the chase begins. Sometimes an animal is big and strong. So the wolves chase it until it gets tired. Then the best hunters move in. They grab the animal from the rear. Another wolf goes for its throat. Sometimes, the animal dies. But sometimes it gets away. And sometimes it even kills a wolf.

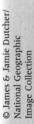

These Yellowstone wolves are on a hunt. Wolves often move in a single file toward an animal they're hunting.

© James & Jamie Dutcher/
National Geographic
Image Collection

A new alpha takes over the pack.
What will happen to Wolf 2?

5

The Last Fight

When Wolf 7 was about eight years old, she was killed by another wild animal. Without Wolf 7, Wolf 2 lost some of his power. Soon, a younger wolf pushed him out of the way and became alpha male.

After that, Wolf 2 spent a lot of time alone. One day, his radio collar sent an alert. Workers could tell that he hadn't

Wolf Packs in Yellowstone

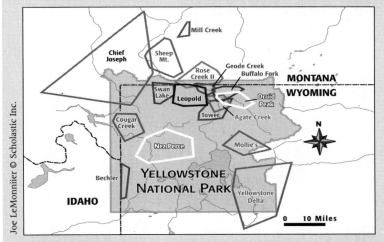

Wolf 2 and Wolf 7 were two of 14 wolves brought to Yellowstone National Park. Now there are about 150 wolves and 14 packs.

moved in five hours. When they found him, he was lying dead in a patch of bloody snow. His body was covered with tooth marks. Wolf 2 had fought hard. But in the end, younger, stronger wolves killed him. They were the new leaders of the pack.

Glossary

alpha *(noun)* a leader of a wolf pack

biologist *(noun)* a scientist who studies living things *(related word: biology)*

den *(noun)* the home of a wild animal

pack *(noun)* a group of wolves

provider *(noun)* someone or something that brings things that are needed

ranchers *(noun)* people who raise cattle, sheep, or horses on large pieces of land

territory *(noun)* an area of land